METAPHYSICS AND MEMORY

Metaphysics
and
Memory

A Poetry Collection

JESSE HAMILTON

RESOURCE *Publications* · Eugene, Oregon

METAPHYSICS AND MEMORY
A Poetry Collection

Resource Publications
An Imprint of Wipf and Stock Publishers
199 W. 8th Ave., Suite 3
Eugene, OR 97401

www.wipfandstock.com

PAPERBACK ISBN: 979-8-3852-1510-2
HARDCOVER ISBN: 979-8-3852-1511-9
EBOOK ISBN: 979-8-3852-1512-6

05/06/24

CONTENTS

INTRODUCTION

I HAVE ALWAYS WRITTEN POETRY; I come by this instinct honestly. Both of my parents love and have written it; my mother still does. I certainly love poetry; I love reading it and writing it, and I have studied and taught it extensively, from middle school to college. None of this qualifies me to publish a collection, of course. We all know people who regularly engage in some art form or another; so many of us have what we might call an "artistic" or "creative" impulse, yet very little of what any of us produce is something that any discernible reader would call great art. Where this collection falls on the spectrum of artistic merit is hard to say; no doubt on the whole it is fairly low, though perhaps at least a few of the poems offer something by way of genuine poetic value (this is no false modesty; after many years of reading and studying great poetry, I am painfully aware of my limitations). There are, to be sure, a wide variety of poetic efforts presented here; some began with lofty poetic aspirations, while others were meant to be nothing more than simple and even sentimental personal reflections. Some are fragments, while others (perhaps a fair number) should have been discarded (as were most of my sonnet efforts, which explains the gaps in numbering); still others were experiments (that no doubt went horribly wrong). After all this, then, why would I seek to publish this collection? Two very simple reasons. First, for posterity; to have my poems in easily accessible form for those who, having some connection to me, may wish to have and regularly read them. Second, because much of my poetry, whatever its lasting worth, deals with what I believe to be significant themes; themes related to ultimate truth and beauty. Each poem attempts to say something of consequence; and such attempts, I believe, are worth reading, provided the author has something to say. The first poem in the collection, for example, "Small Town, USA," critiques a particular (and mostly Southern) brand of Christian nominalism made possible by an aberrant view of the doctrine of grace; "Haiku" offers a reflection on the so-called "aesthetic solution" to the problem of evil; "Moving Day" explores the tension between earthly and heavenly joys; "Holy City" examines the ongoing and damning problem of power and privilege in society and the church; "Death is Never What it Seems" contrasts secular and religious approaches to death (while maintaining, in this case, that "negative capability" Keats wrote of); "Grand Canyon" is essentially a critique of Western society in the modern period; "Autumn Day, 2004" centers on the knowledge of God, occasioned by nature, that human beings experience; etc.

As those close to me will know, I gave up pursuit of a career in philosophy—twice, to be exact—in order to heed a call to ministry. On a different level, then, if I have given up philosophy—my deepest and truest intellectual inclination—why then do I write or seek to publish my poetry? It is a worthwhile question, but I think the answer, again, is fairly straightforward. Philosophy is a rather different undertaking than poetry, requiring time and energy in considerable doses just to read and comprehend it, let alone attempt to write it. Poems, for the most part, require far less time and energy to compose and edit. More significantly, I came to believe that God had called me specifically to give up my study of philosophy, which depends largely on the deliverances of human reason, and instead to pursue spiritual wisdom and effectiveness in ministry; I have not had such a conviction regarding my poetry. To be sure, as I have written elsewhere, God calls those with talents of any sort or scope to give them up entirely to him; he calls us all to surrender everything initially to him, and then to do and pursue only what he calls us to. This is a fundamental requirement of following Jesus. By his grace, I have done so, even with poetry; but I have never felt him call me away from writing it on occasion. I thus hope this very modest collection provides at least some enjoyment and encouragement, and provokes at least some useful reflection, in any and all who read it.

A final note for my fellow Christian readers; you will quickly realize in perusing these poems that some of them make what appear to be surprising statements and deal with rather unsettling thoughts and feelings, including those that occasionally appear to be antithetical to faith. In such poems, I was merely giving voice to what are very real and rather universal human experiences, even (and perhaps especially) among believers. My hope is that such poems will not cause confusion, but rather encouragement. As the Bible itself reveals again and again, to be a Christian is not to live without struggle; the very essence and value of faith lies in its perseverance through the agonizing travails that engender doubt, sorrow, and despair. We could add as well that it is in such suffering, of course, that the most enduring art often emerges.

My thanks goes to Wipf and Stock for publishing this collection; and special thanks, as always, goes to my wife, for whom many of the following poems were written, and who has patiently read and commented on every poem I have attempted over the past 20 years. It is to her, far and away the truest and best artist in the family, that I lovingly dedicate this collection.

I

Metaphysics and Memory

SMALL TOWN, USA

It's just off the interstate
In the middle of nowhere,
This backwoods country town.

Our house sits at the end of a quiet cul-de-sac
That backs up to a three-mile stretch of forest,
Replete with roving herds of white-tailed deer,
Birds of every shade of feather,
And even the mercurial wild turkey
Ducking and bobbing
In misty silhouettes at dawn.

Once, at the far end of the meadow,
An albino doe appeared
Like a portent on the shores of the Mediterranean
In a myth from ancient times,
Then vanished forever, a ghost
To mock our memories.

Sound travels true in these pastoral surroundings.
No pollution pounds the eardrums
And drowns it out; the faintest whisper tiptoes
Lightly along the edges of the cul-de-sac
To the very end of the street
And peeps around the corner
When the air turns light and dry,

And falls quick and heavy like a wounded bird
When the air lies thick.
I like it both ways;
Bits of sentences
Slip as slivers of delicious gossip

Through the splintered web of evergreen branches
As I loll on the patio and peer at my neighbors
From the relative safety of the foliage;
And I can yell anything I want
When the weather's right.

Just outside the neighborhood
Lies a long field where hay is planted.
I cannot tell which time of year I like it best;
In the spring and summer, when the gray-green mottled grass
Stands dense and sprightly
Beneath a cloudless sky,
Or in autumn, when the hay sits tidied
Into trim, neat bundles of wheat and brown
In the orange-tinted temperate afternoon.

Yesterday morning
As the sun beamed boldly in the background,
A low-lying fog hung splendidly
Like a silver halo
Just above the wood-shackled, tin-roofed barn
That sits idly at the back of the field,
And also
Kept company at its feet.
The scene lay ready for safekeeping
With brush and canvas,
But I, possessor of no such tools,
Paused briefly, then moved on,
The sight of it lifting my mood
Like a letter from a long-lost friend.

☼   ☼   ☼

Downtown lies dormant
On the other side of the tracks
In this town just small enough

For both sides to be the same.

The run-down houses remind me
Of something my grandpa once said:
*There's no need to smile
If you're not in the picture.*

Grocery brands thrive here
That long ago were closed down and boarded up
By citizens of the real world.
Emerging from my car
I move carefully to the door.
I grew up in a town like this,
So blending in is easy,
Except for my clothes and my manner.

The pastor of the assembly
On First and Main
Moonlights as the high-school mascot;
It's hard to know which is his disguise,
Or whether man and mask
Are one and the same.

Nevertheless, I greet him warmly,
Sensing that his acceptance of me
Requires far more
Than mine of him.

One might call it irony,
But there is, I suppose, a sort of poetry to the fact
That the oppressive urban sprawls that lie like lava scars
Over all that is organic and green,
Are the only places where one can find
The food of farmers,
While here in the land where it is grown
And where they labor and toil,

One can only find
The mass-produced, manufactured muck
That clogs our valves
And quickens our breath.

Whatever else I feel, the social need
That these quiet haunts
So often meet,
Wherein I whisper quietly to myself
As I move from shelf to shelf
And aisle to aisle—
Captive and insulated
In the eye of the storm—
Betrays me here.

Before me passes
The matron of our neighborhood,
The one who pulls the strings and watches as we
Twitch unnaturally
And cannot be made to stand upright.

Up front, in the check-out line,
Waits the dad whose daughter I teach
At the local Christian school,
Who bristled at the mere suggestion
That free will is an illusion.
My attempt to explain compatibilism
Complete with monographs, slides, charts,
And even polls,
Left him undaunted.
I don't want no PhD candidate in philosophy
He bellowed
Teaching my kids.
I remain to him
A practitioner of secret arts.

I am yet unsure
Whether he has a point,
And whether we're all just better off
Where we belong,
Cocooned
In the weavings of our own wombs.

The check-out girl,
A public high-school student,
Treats me with courtesy;
I note with interest
That she is a local product
And likely to one day leave this place
Never to return.

                    *   *   *

Returning home, I pass
The house that flies the flag
Someone reconfigured
In the latest race conflagration.

My neighbor, the born-again barbecue maestro,
Emerges from his backyard sanctuary
Clutching holy tongs,
Smoke rising from his altar;
He hosts loud parties on Saturday nights
And sleeps in on Sunday mornings.

The buck that was born
Just two summers ago
In the willing grass just beyond my backyard
Halts knowingly, waiting for me to pass;

I wonder if he'll last the season
To be rung in one morning soon
Like an eruption of fireworks
In some pagan festival.

The blood that glazes the early autumn evening sky
Drips on the maple trees,
Glistens at the throat
Of the bullet that buzzes by my brain,
The tongue of which drips with the blood
Of dying flowers;
The blood that blankets everything like snow
In this silent land.

The overstuffed garbage bag
That sits on the lawn
Unties itself and flies away
As two crows; the joke's on me.

It's hard to tell in the gathering darkness
Whether I'm living in
The land that time forgot
Or some godforsaken place

Or somewhere in-between,
So much the worse for me.

HAIKU

Bluebird on a bare
branch in winter; who would put
these two together?

MOVING DAY

The wind whistles
As it rattles
These bare bones,
These clean-picked walls.
All that's left

Are dents, and hidden scars,
And shadowed halls,
Where memories once dangled
And smiles once twinkled
Like distant stars.

The guts of this place,
Its warm and bleeding heart,
Its loves, its laughter,
Its sighs and tears,

Its thoughts, its words,
Its very soul,
Are all gone;
So why

If heaven and home
Are where the heart is,
Am I still clinging to

This silent shell,
This hollow
Hell?

HOLY CITY

So I'm headed down Bay Street coming up on Queen
Watching as the clots of tourists
Coagulate on Cumberland,
Where the sea, with each contraction of its tireless heart
Pumps them daily through the narrow capillaries
Of this hallowed organism,
Raising it to life.
Storefronts lift their droopy lids,
Doors yawn wide and close again
On creaking joints,
While the rhythmic clip-clop of regal hooves
On cobbled stones
Mixes with the resonant hum of laughter
And the vibrant ring of commerce,
As the scent of some unknown spice
Rises on the cloud of the city's thick breath
That seeps from an unseen cavity
Far below
Where the slathery pavement now lies
Hot to the touch.

A right on Broad, a left on Church
And I'm immersed in a garden paradise
Of evanescent glimpses
Of graceful courtyards and noble residences
That close off or fall away
As each successive wall or corner intrudes
And so lie just out of sight.
It was in these inner sanctums
The ubiquitous markers tell us
That worlds once met.
Amid this dazzling maze

11

Of narrow lanes and twisting alleyways
Of varicolored plaster
And impossibly long piazzas
Bedecked with vines and petals
Interwoven into the latticework
Of some exotic style,
Georgian, perhaps, or Federal maybe,
Each stamped with the omnipresent gaslights
That forever burn
In silent memorial,
I can almost get why
In all this impenetrable beauty
And this irresistible grace,
It's hard to hear

The creaking at the dock of the ominous vessel
Hull stained black and rotted from the endless crossings
And the clink of somber chains
And the brazen stares
And the muted whispers
As the ragged souls disembark
And take the lonely march just down the way
To the sullied platform where hearts and lives
Are torn like curtains,

Let alone to remember
That the splendor that once
Broadcast like a beacon from this tiny
Spire-spangled square,
Shone with the brilliant soul-light
That made ghosts of living men.

This is sacred ground, to be sure
But not for the gilded deposition
Of its honor roll of privileged citizens,
But for the forgotten remains
That lie scattered

Along its coastal haunts.

It's all still here,
The imbalanced scale, the cruel indifference,
From the besotted patrons that saturate its streets
To the relentless march of gentrification through its rundown
     quarters
Hey—we want that too,
To the echoes of the gunshots in the sanctuary
Where Dr. King once spoke
So many years ago,
To the invisible wall that still looms large
And sections off
Inch by inch, line by line
Precept by precept—

And I wonder
As I round the storied Battery
And turn again home,
Past the crumbling facades
And the dubious cannons
And the tragic remnant
Out there in the blue somewhere
Of that sibling rivalry
As old as time,

Whether Adam ever gave in to the prevailing urge—
To turn his back upon the broken world
The world that *he* had made,
Tiptoe quietly back inside the fabled walls
Where God once walked,
Shut the imaginary door,
Breathe in again the scent
Of its tainted fruits
And pretend
The whole thing never happened—

DEATH IS NEVER WHAT IT SEEMS

Death is never what it seems
From far away;
The night reminds us, 'till the light
Of cheerful day.

The things that scare us sideways
Resolve at last;
The hurts and wounds all cicatrize
And bind us fast.

The young pine for the moment
The old, the past;
The in-between keep searching
For love at last;

But death is never what it seems
From far away—
Or so says Pastor Robert, as he
Kneels to pray.

GRAND CANYON

Ghosts linger here
In the dank corners and corridors of the lodges
And in the ominous chasm where
Earth and heaven
Never meet.

*   *   *

Away from the busloads of seekers
I take in the wildness of this place
And imagine, far below

Beside the brown thread of river
And the scattered tufts of Douglas-fir,

Hoof strikes, and the occasional
Whisper of worn leather against stone;
The solitary passage of a warrior band
Down the rocky trail.

It will be time again soon
For the mud-paint lines
And the foam of lather
And the bitter grit of spit
And wind-whipped sand
In sun-torched lands;

For the thundering rush—
For the bark-slap *snap*
Of a steel cockscomb hammer sliding into place;

For the gurgling death
And the warwhoop,
As all that thirsty sand
Coagulates inhuman levels
Of warm, rich blood;

But now there is only
The gentle curl of water
And the intermittent wingbeats
Of a condor,

Above these mottled walls
That alternately
Hide and frame them.

☆　☆　☆

Tonight, that one will take
The ocotillo from his soles, and kneel
Obediently between the knees of his one woman,
And tomorrow

He will rise, cat-limbed, and wrap
His hide-bound cloak
Around his naked flesh, and stand
Together with the spires of morning smoke

In perfect silence
Toward the rising sun.

I HAVE FELT SIN BEFORE

I have felt sin before,
The kind that clasps you in its virulent clutches,
The vile, impenetrable hold that no man
Can break, the grip that kills;

But now, sin has been killed in me,
And it no longer threatens.
Though it still jumps and flutters,
These are merely

The last, faint stirrings of a lifeless corpse;
The nerveless twitches of a dead man;
The ghostly jerks and shudders
Of a soul reborn.

ROAD

A poem in nine kennings

Stall-ender
Mind-bender
Soul-mender.

Mood-wearer
Grief-sharer
Hope-bearer;

Heart-blender
Time-stealer
Fate-sealer.

AUTUMN DAY, 2004

Within a quiet wood today,
Behind some unknown hill,
There came upon me such a scene
My soul could not keep still.

It happened in the evening time
My heart was heading home
When there it broke upon my view
And begged my soul to roam.

I had no cause upon that day
To lose a single hour—
Yet still the scene encompassed there
Enclosed me in its power—

A silent stream wound gently through
A sea of gold and red;
The boughs dropped final patches on
Their richly-quilted bed;

A solemn hush no sound had stirred
The stream no sole had trod—
The stillness fairly echoed with
The boundless voice of God.

The sun sank down, the light was gone,
But still I sit and think
From time to time, of all the truth
This world displays and tells;

Our thoughts and words betray us, but
Our feelings never do;
I'll trust my heart to lead me home
Until my day is through.

CHARTER SCHOOL

Bike wheels wobble
And fall off, here where
The air is dusty
The road worn
And fresh generations of illegals learn
To duck and dodge.

You don't feel much like talking
When you're tasting
The same bitter weeds
That Nebuchadnezzar nibbled, here
Where the sun don't shine.

Backhoes and strip bars slouch
Side by side, beside
The overpass.
It's hard to pass over
The filth:

I watch as a homeless man walks by
With his crotch open, manhood lagging
Like a memory;
He has somewhere to go.

Outside these walls
Dopers and hookers lounge,
Looking to score,

While inside
A charter school principal pleads
For more donations from home,
Then roars off

In a chrome-plated Hummer,
Exhaust sitting thick and choking
The life out of
An otherwise pristine scene.

BEFORE AND AFTER

A Bildungsroman

I remember well those August days,
Ideals lagging like vowels
In the lurid Louisiana heat;

Wafting, wisp-like, in the cool early morning hours
But burned down by noon
To their pure lust core.

Limbs laboring clumsily through cobwebs of sweat;
Sin clinging close like a lathery lover.

My grandfather, larger than life
Ruled two terms of government
Over that vast domain,
Then came home to carve his growing legend
Onto the earth's own face. Each time we visited
He made us tour his burgeoning crop-fields
On otherwise barren afternoons.
We grew numb watching the endless ranks flecked white with
    cotton
File past our dusty jeep
As he surveyed the plantation grounds
Like a demagogue.

He cast a long shadow
Over those sun-drenched autumn fields.
No child would dare outrun it;
The only game was to try
To secretly mingle one's own shadow with his,
The thrill of merging
Into a frame so much bigger than one's own.

I was 22 when the legend died.
By then I was high in the stratosphere
Headed East at supersonic speeds
To some other far-off, mystical place, to live out
Some new kind of fantasy.
When that, too, ended,
I came home.

*   *   *

Untold days deleted
Like worn-out story prompts.

To walk
The dusty plains where ambition once flowered;
To taste
The bitter grit of years irretrievable;
To face
One's truth;
To lead
One's own shadow across an open plain;

To tremble
With the knowledge of what might have been,
Had one only known
How all things end

In time.
They disappear and die
Like objects in a lucid dream
Upon waking,

The myth, the land, the sky—
The eternal I.

THE UNFORGIVEN

Bless you, Audrey Hepburn
For your doe-eyed innocence
And your reed-thin waist
And the raven's wing of thick hair
Cascading down your unbowed back
Like midnight rain, eyes shimmering in the foreground
Like the faith in John Huston's star-spangled soul;
Bless you for your elegant sincerity.

I, however, will not be seduced
By the rapturous sight
Of Burt Lancaster's cliff-hewn brow
And crag-covered hands
Cradling your tender, dovelike face
In the thrill of twice-forbidden romance
Realized,
While the war-drums hum—

Anti-racism flick my ghostly-white soul.

I will be satisfied when the script is flipped—
When I'm scorching popcorn to the sight
Of Burt Lancaster looming in the burning doorway
Searching for his long-lost sister
And suing for peace,

When a broken-off lance of bitterness
Sends his shapeless, forked-tongue soul
Straight to the afterlife swift
As the falcon falls.

THE HUMMINGBIRD

The hummingbird hovers
Over the palo verde tree,
Measuring
Its gilded hem.

It zips down of a sudden
Then pauses,
Extending its needle-like bill
To fix a tremulous style.

It does not pierce
The fragile heart.
It need not penetrate,
Yet still gives life

Even as it suckles,
Replacing
As it uses:

Pollen for nectar,
Seed for blood.

On this lazy summer day
The air is balmy
The city is at peace

And nature is so much more
Than it appears.

THE WORLD MOVES BY

The world moves by at its own frantic pace;
I am in it but not of it.
The ceaseless hum
Of mindless traffic, noise without words,
Mars the gentle song inside my window.

When will it end, this maddening malaise,
This barbarous hunger
Of the middle class?
Infectious pests, devouring horde,

Swooping down to leafy green
And virgin bud,
And whittling them to stalk.
Breeding. Breeding. Breeding.

                              *   *   *

Bare, brittle blow the reeds,
Tender shoots long fractured by the summer sun,
Pale silhouettes faintly shifting in the autumn breeze;
Waiting on the long, hard freeze of winter
And shadowy death.

Lonely, silent lie the watering places,
Shrunken are the pools, dry as the brakes that fed them;
Humble are the livestock, lowly at heart;
Not even death lives here, there's no need for it now.

Lo, gather around me, children!
Come hither with me, let us look on death;
It lies not where lost souls in the churchyard are gathered—
It lives where the glutted saint bares his breath.

THE STORM IS COMING

Upon a Reading of J.C.R.

The God who thunders
Thunders still,
But in more subtle ways.

He thundered first
Upon the hill
And down through ancient days;

He even spoke
Quite recently
Through some of our own kind—

But prophets ceased
Some time ago
To be in their own minds.

Yet this is no
Alarm for those
Who still hold out for rain;

Who wish the heavens
To relieve
The harsh and bare terrain;

Bend low thine ear
To earth, my friend
And hear its heart a humming—

Just because
The sky is clear
Doesn't mean the storm's not coming.

A LIFE LOST

A soft answer
Doesn't always turn away wrath;
Ask Him.

Neither does love unremitting
Always keep back
The wayward soul.

                    *   *   *

We grew up apart in age and gender,
Yet of the same fabric, the same
Life-code;
Similar enough in outlook and essence
To pass through different cycles in life
And remain intertwined
As friends.

Fate directed us down different paths,
Each with its own set of values and symbols,
Yet not unalike in form,
Separated here and there by mere syllables;

The lengthening of a line here;
The broadening of a stroke there;

The addition of a simple proposition or two
Resulting in
The sum of all arguments.

I was convinced
That the way you were taking

Would lead only to misery,
Yet not even I could anticipate
The depth of horror
You would one day feel.

Left alone to experience
The enormity of true loss,
The sudden passing of soul, a cleavage
Unmitigated by the slightest gradation of strangeness,
The simultaneous realization in full
Of emptiness and ungratified empathy;

Bereft of all hope
When hope
Was at its most sincere;

And helpless at the last
(And here is where the real pain comes in),
To be of any use whatsoever
To either body or soul;

A life lived so long undermining
Words uttered for the first time;

A signpost
So far removed from its place
To be of no use
To the one who reads it.

And so a life was lost.

✳   ✳   ✳

Where the fire burns blackest,
Where the soil rubs clean, giving way to dust,
There can be no replowing

Or replanting of seed,
But only the abandonment of that place
To the whims of the wind.

And yet in the midst of such tragedy
You found some lesson, some reason
For hope;
A glimmer of light among the indefatigable shadows;
A murmur of truth in the deafening silence.
And there, at last, we found this common ground:

That despite all things,
Eventually we unlearn the myth
That Providence, like a gin,
Only tears so far as to separate
Flower from seed;
The former harvested, stitched together,
And worn to the world;
The latter not discarded,
But gathered, replanted,
And tended as fruit.

For how can one navigate the heart?
How can one circumscribe,
How can one ever dead reckon
With the way one feels?

And yet we are left alone to pilot
These treacherous waters that turn
Every which way upon us,
No matter how they flow.

And thus were you caught up again into that current;
Thus were you again rebuffed by the tide;
Thus were you swept out once more to sea
To drift along and be picked up

By the first vessel unencumbered enough
To uncoil its line.

❊   ❊   ❊

It may be the plucking
Of a tightly wound string
That sounds the virtuous note;
But that same persistent plucking
Day after day
Will wear the wire thin
Until it breaks.

This alone I have learned,
That so often in life,
More often perhaps than one's faith is brave enough to admit,
The easy way does not lead to destruction,
Nor the hard way into any sort of
Translatable joy.

If there is indeed a reconciliation of these,
If there is indeed a justice of sorts,
It is far, so far ahead of us,
That it does no good to strain the eye
Or even imagine it there,
But merely to sit back and ride out the undistractable
Motion of time.

❊   ❊   ❊

Of the little that remains between us,
Among the many things that I will take away,
I only know that I can never forget
The imposing, other-worldly blackness of that day;

32

How you folded your arms and laughed as I struggled
Under the cumbersome
Weight of your weakness;

How you left my soul
Hanging there,
Hurt driven into my heart
Like a spear.

SCIENCE: A REBUTTAL

I stand before science with shield aside and sword drawn;
I defy that it wields anything to conquer me.

This so-called proof today is lapped by intellectual cubs;
Innocent; naïve; tender; prey;
Too keen to cut their teeth upon
An unsuspecting world.

I will not be held back by such watery nourishment.
I cast it all aside as one robust and strong;
I pound my hairy fist upon the bar and roar
For meat upon my table.

I cannot believe in the claims of modern science
Anymore than I can disbelieve
In the infinite fecundity and potential of you;
Even you the most inert and unfruitful of souls.

That the smallest living cell,
Or piece of matter, or whatever is needed to postulate,
Could ever morph, over a million years,
Into the limitless faculty we call the human mind;
The very thought that one day we could stand over nature
And all of lesser life
And call it our creator, in a sense
More bizarre yet real than we have heretofore been willing to
        admit,
Is not only outside the limits of reason and of all good sense,
But sheer impossibility.

So too, the possibility
That I, upon a given day,

Through absolute randomness fashioned to an nth degree of
    exactness,
Of quiet molecule, chemical, energy,
Protein, cell, tissue and water,
Could focus without thought and with unconscious precision
Upon a single object built with the same stuff and yet with such
An entirely disassociated result,
A growth, a flower,

And that its code of splendid form and brilliant color
Which alone can be translated and processed by me,
Would so fascinate me,
Hold me in place, leave me without breath,
Transfix my mind,
Leave its imprint on
My soul,
And fill me with the strange, intoxicating odor
Of immortality.

There can be no other conclusion but that
Not only was I fashioned to walk upright,
To search and wander, and finally
To see this thing,
But also that it was left on purpose
For me to find,

A hint, a clue,
A trail of notes,
Leading to the top of some remote and distant mountain,
Far, far above the wind and rain, the vicissitudes of earth,
And every shifting thought,

For me to stand upon a solid peak
And stare into an endless sky,

Straining to see,
Waiting to hear.

FALLING

I have seen human souls in various stages of decomposition;
Smiles stretched tautly and awkwardly over face bones
Like plastic wrap over the remains
Of Sunday lunch;

Where conversations, picked over
Once lay blood-boiling and simmering with promise;
Now dry as bone, like passion
Through lack of temperance, the inexorable effects
Of heat and empty time.

I have traveled old roads
Once full of joy and replete with promise,
Reveling in the sure destination of coming years;
Now turned to stone and redirected,
Small pathways overcome simultaneously
By progress and neglect;
No longer poignant or purposeful for exploration
By human traffic.

They leave a void, these memories,
Especially when paired with the awful knowledge
Of how time tempers and moves on;
How dreams, once vivid, are never realized;
How the mind grows old, the passions wither,
And the cords of faith, like youth,
Might one day snap and fall away

—While so many around are still caught up
In the mindless rush
Of mid-day heat,
Whose seed-like souls one day too soon

Will too dry up and blow away,
But only after

Hope and all the shimmering ideals
The heart takes hold of
Then releases,
As it falls down dead
And still beats on—

SPRING BAYOU

The wind still whispers through the Long Field,
Rattling the reeds with gentle promises,
Bearing the scent of things to come, new air,
Stirring the heart to yearn for yesterday.

My father spent his childhood on a tract of land
Alongside the Tensas, its wood and wildlife
One and the same;

Where the last of the Lord God Birds was spotted
Clinging to a worn-out cypress stump,
Whittling down time.

My father, as man was made,
Passed whole days in solitude,
Moving through the woods as both
King and caretaker;

Seeing the bobbing flocks of turkey
Acknowledge and take flight, their wing beats
Swift and sure against the evening air.

Snakes of all stripes slipped past
Or wound in warning; black bear lolled
Somewhere far off; deer flagged white
And trotted, unafraid;

Birds spread paint upon the canvas sky
And whistled.

When at last the urban sprawl
Overruns the soul, as always it will
—Just as the human heart
Alone, can never tip the balance toward
Caution or restraint—

There quickly wither
All the organic places of the heart,
Turning to stone
Like the sprawling edifices of death
That bruise the landscape;

Its hides and hollows smashed or filled;
Its tender shoots uprooted;
Its vines that climbed and twisted
Ripped and pulled down;
Its fertile soil
Laid flat, and turned to
Barren road;

Its melodic language
Hushed and drowned
By the harsh and cutting noise
Of humankind.

RESOLUTION

I'm through with conscience and its prudish ways,
That nosy-eyed neighbor in curlers and bathrobe
Peeping through the curtains of the heart
Never leaving well enough alone
And never quite aware enough
To keep from being caught.

I will not dwell in fear.
I will roam, naked and carefree
Of soul, from room to room of life
With windows wide; not out of spite, not in
Amoral flaunt or show; but with such decency, such grace
That she at last will draw the shade, and blushing turn away.

THE MORNING AFTER

If the soul finds, upon waking
That the dense and bristled overgrowth
That once shaded its paler lines and weaker features
From the sheer light of day

Has all been plucked clean,
Leaving a feel
Too raw, too bare
Upon reflection,

It is enough.
What's needed merely
Is the balm of possibility
In the hands of time.

There's just no sense
In running over it all again
With the ragged
Razor of regret.

TRUTH

Truth is an unsuspecting citizen
Arraigned on the slimmest of charges.
All one needs is a pot-bellied hunch
And pressure to crack the case.

BELIEF

Belief, in itself,
Is fundamentally undependable.

The reason is,
That belief, like reason,
Is tautly yet firmly bound
To the feelings.

It can be tugged on and tossed around
By every wind of thought;
But wherever the heart is anchored,
There it moors.

Like the mother who just can't believe her child did that;
Like the rival who's been waiting for you to mess up
And just knows you did;

Like the fear that leads to faith
Or the anger
That destroys it.

It's not that truth doesn't exist;
It's out there, beaming a perfect signal.

The heart is a just terribly ill-equipped device
For drawing it in.

CLASSICAL HIGH SCHOOL HISTORY CLASS. TWO AUTUMN AFTERNOONS STITCHED TOGETHER.

My lectures are the most powerful sedative in the world.
Outside our window, a block of wood
Sits suspended on a sagging power line
That stretches toward some unknown tree
And disappears into its clouded foliage.
We do not know how it got there
But we care.
That matters, on a day when ancient glory
Rots like a bloated carcass on the bleached shores
Somewhere far below
Our washed-out horizons.

A breakthrough.
The drone of class
Is interrupted by the far more ecstatic drone
Of an unidentifiable winged creature
Come to suck our blood.
Its naked thickness
Sends this class of mostly female souls
Into a tizzy.
Caleb, lone descendant of the gods
(He bleeds the Percy Jackson series),
Frees some unread commentary of its dust jacket,
Enters the side room where the creature has unwittingly flown
And locks the door behind him.
We wish him well.

My life is the two-dimensional map
That sits wrinkled

On the wall beside me,
Together with the smiling Henry James
That the students depressingly say
Reminds them of me. He was probably a genius, I remind them,
But this fact is sadly undetectable
In the Singer portrait.
He could be anybody or everybody
And has already been redesignated
As everyone's least favorite uncle.
I think he looks judge-like,
Presiding over
The crowded courtroom that is our class,
Complete with U-shaped table
And jury of our peers. He may condemn us,
But we do not care;
He's already been executed.
Guilty, we turn our steely gaze
To other great ones of the past.
We judge everyone but ourselves;
They are guilty too.

Heavens, how we need
That third dimension
In this world that's somehow
Gone flat again.
I try
To steer them back to ancient lands,
Lead tours of crumbled ruins,
Unveil their glory, inspire them
To topple fabled monuments, run their own races
And win some mythic prize,
But inevitably
Their minds are conquered
By lowly distant thoughts.
Anything will do.
AP Bio

Has lobotomized the spirit out of
The last few survivors
Of our crowded days,
As AP Bio
Is wont to do.
I'd like to murder
AP Bio.

My *School of Athens*
Which has survived unscathed these odd years
Feels as if
It belongs in a dusty photo
Of a time when people cared about
Good art. We read
From a book of modern poetry,
But lose interest when
The cows start talking. Or rather
We perk up
Losing interest in
The art of poetry
But wanting more cow.
One wore sunglasses,
For heaven's sake;
That's something I can take with me
When school lets out.
The weary hum
Of cars outside our window
Makes matters worse;
We cannot tell
Whether they are coming or going.
The day could not degrade
Much further,
When Caleb returns

Holding proof of his mastery over
His medieval thick boy.

He strides like some Colossus o'er
The humble realm of our classroom
Lofting it by its broken wing.
He lays it across his palm
And strolls around
For us to admire. This is his moment.
At least
Something has died, I sigh;
That's something.
The sighs
When we return to thought
Make me feel sympathy.
My lectures are the most powerful sedative in the world,
And I would rather
Hear myself than them;
But there is no need
To push them further.
Life will do that
Soon enough.
I try
To redeem the moment
By suggesting we turn this mundane afternoon
Into a poem,
But there is no hope;

I haven't taught them how. We've only
Wandered into nature on some vacant trail
In days gone by,
Searching for something which no longer
Seems alive; something forbidden, something
Quaint, something
Anachronistic, maybe;
Love, or hope, or joy,
Or even God.
Some of us say we've found it
But struggle to keep it.

Others
Never bothered.
There will be other flies
To catch, on other afternoons
To get through, and maybe
Just maybe, we can stitch together enough of these
To weave ourselves some twisting reach of rope
Climb upward toward that gaping skylight
In the corner of the musty ceiling
And blow this joint.

NOSTALGIA

Where did yesterday already go,
When the frames of life click slow, slow;
And static scenes of pleasures past
Always never seem to last?

There is no joy in things to come;
The pain of loss is all we'll know;
One simple thing alone shall last—
These moments that so quickly pass.

I CAUGHT A GLIMPSE

I caught a glimpse
Of my mortality today,
And felt as if upon a stream
Just up from where the final bend
Unveils the bay,
And saw, beyond the silent deep
That ever-glowing parting line
Of night and day.

In just a little while, I thought,
Our lives will end,
And no one knows the how, the why,
Or when,
But only that a little while,
And then

We'll know how much our lives below
Held back the flow of others
Like the tide,
Or billowed out their spirits
Like the wind.

II

Six Vignettes, China

CHINESE COLLEGE CLASSROOM, KUNMING

It sure doesn't look like Communism here,
What with the erratic confection
Of really bad hairdos,
The art of Burmese immigrants stuck
In 1982, punk spikes, thick chains
And all,

Strands limp, lifeless
With the inclement November weather,
The favored color some
More optimistic red,

Japanese, or Korean, maybe—
Anything but black.

KUNMING RIVER

A river flows through the middle of Kunming,
Sparkling and clear down to its depths
In its upper-most reaches, out where peasants draw
Its life-giving coolness to sun-parched lips;

But as it moves through this crowded city of men,
Its waters darken, turning with each bend
A shade more green,
Until at the last its muck-thick dregs
Resolve into a toxic tarn.

It's sad—lamentable, one should say—
That a river, like the flow
Of good intentions,
Might run pure clean to its length—
Mind you, from lofty
Source to mouth—
If it didn't run right through
The heart of town.

DURING A VISIT TO THE WILD ANIMAL PARK, KUNMING

The lion on the knoll, a mass
Of rippling strength,
Of monumental frame, and granite bone,
Of splendid muscle, chiseled, taut and lean,
Of razor tooth and claw, and fearsome gaze,
Of ragged mane and worn-out, dusty hide,
In perfect silence sits, composed, unmoved
By all below.

He pays no heed to me, or to
The silly antics of less civil creatures—
We who ape and dance before
His regal form.
He does not move a bit, or feel
The least alarm;
His tail alone, with dull twitch, here, and there,
Belies his calm—

While we around the chain-link stare,
Captivated, freed—
Subdued by righteous dread, and yet
Wild with savage glee.

RICKSHAW ROUNDUP

Wasteland of shattered panes and twisted metal;
Wheels, those matchless measures of real time
Forever frozen in silent air;

The sight of justice served;
Law's long arm bared; or

Souls o'er-turned,
Lives upended.

WENCHUAN

Five times I've felt the earth flutter
In this faithless town, each time the jolt
Unhinging the backbone, leaving the soul
Likewise displaced; fear dislodging
For but a moment,
Foundations as deep as those
Beliefs are built on.

Once, the shudder
Broke old buildings apart, not very far away,
Crushing tens of thousands of tiny
Thoughts and dreams down on
Still-beating hearts,
Years left
To bleed out in the broken soil.

The sentient soul, left standing,
Writhes under the unspeakable weight
Of all those shattered lives,
Pain reverberating
Like aftershocks of terror
In a worn-out mind,

And knows
That the only way to redeem the soul
Of all that loss,
Is to lay one's own life down over
That tremulous fault line
That still rings the world,

Dividing
Love from every life unshaken
By deep disturbances
Of human joy.

LITTLE QIN QIN

Little Qin Qin is a naughty girl,
Self-willed, rebellious, clever;
We cannot make her sit or stay;
Wash and eat; rest or pray.

"Get down, little Qin Qin;
NO, little Qin Qin;
Qin Qin, say you're sorry;
Qin Qin, come with me."

Little Qin Qin is a naughty girl,
Wishing all to see;
But only when she wants to show
And never when we need to know.

"Qin Qin, how many times have I told you?
Now is not the time for that.
Little Qin Qin, say you're sorry.
Qin Qin, come with me."

Little Qin Qin is a naughty girl
But then, she's only three;
She has no parents that we know
And nowhere else to be;

"Grandma," a street-wise local crook
Found her and took her in;
Then burned her face so she could beg—
Scarred her from ear to chin.

"It's okay, little Qin Qin, I can tell
What it is you wish to say;
You'll speak much better when you're grown—
All you need is practice."

"Run and play, little Qin Qin, run, run, run!
Hide well! Don't let them find you.
I've got you, little darling, you won't fall.
Jesus loves you, precious. Jesus loves you."

III

Selected Sonnets

A PRAYER

Dear God, when I in error go astray
And seek for that which transient pleasure brings—
Those thrills of earth, those fickle, short-lived things
Which hush or scatter at my darkening way;
Forgetting that the path ahead displays
Thy greater glory, and thy grander power;
Exchanging, for the fortunes of an hour
The never-ending treasures of thy grace;
Then take me, Father, as a wandering babe
Who, though strong-willed or nescient, yet is blessed
When plucked from snarling traffic, swift and safe,
And scolded not, nor chided like the rest;
But with thy tender, child-like cry of praise
Is folded soft and gentle to thy breast.

SONNET 13

Upon reading of the death of Shelley and the discovery of a volume of Keats's poetry in his pocket

Of all the tales of glory that survive
The struggles of life's bravest and its best,
One small discovery towers o'er the rest
Like snow-crowned peak to barren mountainside.
Dear God! I never dreamed of fame so high,
To be, when Shelley finished out his quest
And lay, victorious, flung out from the crest
Found 'neath his brave and battered soul to lie—
Yet all life's glory, Lord, but ebbs to thee.
I'd rather stand unnoticed in thy lines
And gain one spot in thine eternity
Than live the full of life in this world's mind
Like noble Keats, whose patron through the raging sea
Washed up immortal on the strand of time.

SONNET 18

*Upon parting from a friend and passing
through the minefields of Kunming*

But once, in all of life's bare-chiseled hours
There gleams a gilded moment, when a glance
Cast out in time, led by some fabled powers,
Strikes haply on some like mind, left by chance
To lift thy common fate. If this be so
In thine own life, then be it friend or love
Thy days shall pass, though brief, on earth below
As rich as ceaseless years in heaven above.
Friend, thou didst give this doggerel to me.
Though love be not our lot, as we do lie
Apart in faith, and soon, in strange and distant lands
We shall be separate; yet, let now this plea
Be honored: That in thine heart, as in mine
Our friendship firm shall hold, 'till fate re-clasp our hands.

THE CRITIC

Where truth has gone, no one can say. I hear
There's music still, and poetry, more or less;
There's art on walls, or so it would appear
If judging by the patrons and the press;
They hand out prizes still, and shake the hands
Of all the best of those inclined to try;
Then draw the shades, and cough up new demands
And watch as dreams and inspiration die.
I say it's an illusion. Truth has gone
Somewhere far off; I'll wager, too, that art,
Unknown to all its trade, has followed suit.
Each needs the other. Neither, when alone
Can bear the awful distance when apart;
Art is a flower. Truth its withered root.

SONNET 27

A reply to moral skepticism

There are things that matter and things that don't
In this grand and great big world of ours;
There are those who will, there are those who won't
In the heat of life's embattled hours.
There's a voice that is calling, there's a sound
To be heard, just over the empty noise
Of time; there's a destiny waiting, around
The bend—a single, solitary choice.
There are things to be done, things left to chance
If only the human heart were willing
To take a broad leap into empty space
With the strength once struck numb by only a feeling;
To stand between fate and circumstance—
To rise and be counted; to take one's place.

SONNET 32

Upon the sudden passing of an acquaintance

We're all just a stone's throw away from death;
Our lives like the mindless toe-flick of a pebble;
An instant from when that last infant-like breath
Is sucked out of life by the mother of evils.
It could come whisk-like in a moment of hurry
The last destination en route to the mind;
Or it could be the end of a death-load of worry
That unending, soul-wasting, deathly-slow kind.
It could be one of a million things
But the truth is we act like we're living forever—
Even though for so many the last moment brings
A lifetime of heart-rending regrets together.
The hardest of things for a body to do
Is to live in the now like the not yet is true.

SONNET 35

A take on Emerson's use of the phrase

The apple never falls very far from the tree;
That is, until some wise guy comes along
And kicks it, just like somebody did me
And sends it tumbling toward the open sea.
So many roads out there, it's hard to choose,
But it only takes one bad one to ruin the bunch;
There's shiploads of danger, skin can easily bruise;
So much to gain, and so much to lose.
The apple never falls very far from the tree,
And it's a big old world, there's a lot to learn;
But down at the core, if the roots went deep
The heart will be struck with a homeward yearn—
And no matter how far, it will always come 'round
To that first gentle grove, and its love-lush ground.

SONNET 37

On Hogan Plantation

It still sings, that haunting, hallowed song,
The one that carried multitudes along
In steel-clad courage, blinding in the light
Into the darkness of that long, gray night.
It still is heard, that hymn too full for words
The one that only heart and heaven heard
As evening slowly ripened into night
And all the world grew silent at the sight.
But I shall wait where ghostly trees still sway
Their gnarled and knotted strands of negro gray;
Where progress still is pained by hobbled knees
Like those that bore a thousand sacred pleas;
The pleas that rose unheeded with the wind—
The wind that comes and calls, and never ends.

SONNET 38

There are two kinds of people in the world,
If ever such a statement could be true;
There are those who travel with flag unfurled
And land wherever conscience tells them to;
And there are those who aim for certain spots
And strain wheel and rudder to get them there,
Not able to pass by the crowded lots
Or willing on truth's whim to take a dare.
And on such islands occupied by these
Who huddle en masse, and move as one,
The talk is only what aims to please,
Not what is needed, nor what must be done;
And if there wanders in a soul alone
He is stripped, beaten, and made to atone.

SONNET 39

Christmas, 2018

"Where is He who has been born King of the Jews? For we saw His star in the east and have come to worship Him."

—MATTHEW 2:2

Held back—kept hidden in some ancient fold
Of inky solitude, in distance space—
Then called! Lit boldly, with a burning face
To blaze the greatest story ever told!
O silent star! O pure, O radiant light!
That fixed a startled gaze, that led a curious mind
Into the scene the prophets longed to find—
Light of the world, born to our hopeless night!
Fair Jesus! Savior of mankind! A babe
Wrapped in the fabric of his own dear earth;
Behold the shining face, the tender head!
Come down, the whole wide firmament to save;
The unseen hand, the pained, inglorious birth—
His smile our joy, his cry—life from the dead!

SONNET 40

At Bradford Meadow, Mebane, NC
Composed upon a September afternoon,
on the occasion of my 40th birthday

Just where the winding path turns to the road
Beside the bark-stripped birch, nestled between
Two stands of poplar; there, unheard, unseen,
I sat, while life and time's cruel engine slowed.
Fair meadow! Mender of my fractured heart,
Unspoiled by sound, secured by fragrant trees;
Graced here and there by birds, and gentle breeze
Up where the earth and silent heavens part—

Cruel evening! Stealer of my light and soul,
Casting thy widening shadow o'er the wall
That shields my refuge; agent of dark night!
How can I face the fears that on me roll
As day's last hours and hopes before me fall,
And all these tender joys fade out of sight?

IV

Poems for Ana

SONNET TWO

To Ana, written during our courtship

In earth's dry regions daytime yields a heat
That no green plant or flower can endure;
Yet when rain comes, the moisture is so sweet
That desert flowers bloom in bright allure.
Out o'er the ocean, winds can wield a storm
That ships of men could never overcome;
But when the sun breaks out, all bright and warm
The soul feels peace like to arriving home.
Just so in life. When lone in desert hours
Love's pure refreshment can the soul revive;
And when life's tempest threatens to devour
Love brings a calm that lets the soul survive.
Dear girl, your love's more rich and dear to me
Than rain to dust, or rest to troubled seas.

TO MY WIFE, DECEMBER, 2006

The treasure that I hunted for
At last I found;
Half-hidden in a shallow dent
Of fallow ground;

It lay perceptible unto
The naked eye;
Yet none (thank God) was bare enough
Who passed it by;

Now, nights and nights on end I sit
Content to be
A miser to the clinking of
Eternity;

Some hoard their fame or circumstance,
And some their gold—
But I, the brilliance of your bright
And perfect soul!

VERSES WRITTEN TO MY WIFE
ON HER BIRTHDAY, 2007

This world's a cold, dark place, where lie the shorn
And bare and tattered souls left out to die;

The jagged jaws of snarling fate have torn
To pieces all whose scent it happened by;

Your heart's a quiet hearth, where till the morn
In its warm and flick'ring love-light I shall lie.

AFTERWARDS

Surrendering myself to you,
Knowing you fully
Just as I
Am fully known,

Is to scale the heights of some
Vast, unattainable peak,
Towering in my imagination—

A thrill,
A dare,
A need.

Gazing into your soul afterwards,
Like the view from the top,
Is not the aim itself,
Nor the accomplishment,
But is, still, its own reward—

A confirmation of sorts;
The fond, peaceful remembrance
Of what was sought.

TO MY WIFE BEFORE THE BIRTH OF OUR FIRST CHILD

It was there that I first saw your face,
In that old and run-down shopping-center parking lot,
On that hot and blinding July summer day.
As you stepped face-first into the sun,
The day grew pale and bland before
The rich and pure-cream white of your porcelain skin
Together with the dusty-blue shade of your eyes that matched.
I remember trying to count the splash of freckles on your nose,
And wondering if any more were coming out that moment in the
     sun;
But more than anything else I remember the smile that lit
That corners of your mouth, then danced into your eyes,
Just like the distant sparkle of a summer ray
Far, far from all that concrete and the glass
Upon a clear, blue lake.

You could not know it then, but as you smiled,
I saw, or felt, that very moment,

The heated rush of bodies intertwining,
The ecstatic thrill of two unfettered souls
Struggling to unite;
The heave of weary heartbeats, one upon another;
That deep, unconscious sleep
That only lovers know;
The smell of day's first light, and its first
Naked blushes;
And all the joy we birthed there—all the joy
Which we now wait upon.

All this I saw,
That brief and timeless moment that you stepped
Into the sun.

Then I smiled back
(If you remember),
Knowing what I knew
And that
You did not know.

SONNET 33
To My Wife, April, 2009

There's no such thing in the world as love;
Not really; not the kind that lasts or stays;
There's nothing so divine, no gift from above
That bears all ills 'til the end of days;
Love's not a scheme of its own design;
It has no ethereal power of its own;
But springs from a source entombed in time
And flows through earthy flesh and bone.
Yet all of the love a man can give—
All this and more I have given to you;
So now let us look up to where love lives
In its final state, where its ends are true;
That place where wounded hearts are made whole
If but one beat sounds in the prostrate soul.

SONNET 41

For Ana On Her 35th Birthday

The trees sag wearily about the lawn;
The sun sinks with a melancholy hue;
Our doe limps slowly by with one less fawn
Needing to rest until the night is through;

The hummingbirds have fled to warmer climes;
The leaves lie dormant on the fading grass;
The soul sends up a sigh for fairer times
As if to stall the future with the past—

Ahead lies winter with its deathly chill
And darkness with its terrifying might.
But let all die, and time bring what it will—
My heart will guard its embers through the night;

No matter what remains, or what will be—
Your love has been the difference to me.

FOR ANA

You can't stop gravity, can hardly
Slow it down;
The swift and fiery plunge of objects
To the ground;
The sweep of twisting planets
'Round the sun;
The tug of drifting bodies
One to one.

I wasn't born to stay at home, but far
To wander;
Roaming wide in distant spaces
Way out yonder;
And I did, 'till nudged by forces great and old
Into the ethereal orb that rings your soul.

Now do I trace a sure and steady path,
No more to swerve, or stray outside your love;
Not bound by space, nor meant in time to be undone;
But free in one unending arc
To run and run.